The
Gu

Playing Out

Philip Waters

The Buskers Guide to Playing Out

ISBN - 1-904792-16-2
© Philip Waters 2006

Illustrations © Chris Bennett 2006

Published by Common Threads Publications Ltd.
Wessex House
Upper Market Street
Eastleigh
Hampshire SO50 9FD.
T: 07000 785215
E: info@commonthreads.co.uk

Other titles in The Buskers Guide series include;
The Buskers Guide to Behaviour
The Buskers Guide to Inclusion
The Buskers Guide to Playwork
The Buskers Guide to Anti-Discriminatory Practice

The text of 'The Buskers Guide...' series can be made available in 14 point font – please contact the publishers by telephoning 07000 785215 or emailing info@commonthreads.co.uk

The Buskers Guide to Playing Out

Contents

Introduction

When I was about ten years old, two friends and I went to play on a housing construction site. We found this large wooden crate that resembled a coffin and so took it in turns to lie inside and have the lid closed on us. Cruel though it may seem now, two of us sat on the lid while the third was inside and pretended we were never going to let him out. We did of course, and for the rest of that evening we played vampires and vampire hunters, even sharpening a few sticks for good measure.

It was also around this age that I remember playing in a cattle market opposite our junior school. We would climb over the railings and swing on the large gates, and one older boy would climb onto the roof of the cattle sheds. On one occasion he fell through the old asbestos sheeting and hit the floor rather awkwardly. He was taken away in an ambulance but he was ok.

If another memory serves me correctly, myself and other children from our housing estate would regularly engage in 'tag' or hide-and-seek games, but often to the horror of elderly people because we would use the alleyways between their bungalows as hiding places, the noise probably scaring the hell out of them. We probably also cherry-knocked a few as well!

Another memory from my childhood was that a few of us would play a game that involved one person walking backwards across a road while pretending to unwind a drum of wire. The general idea was to make the approaching car driver believe that we were laying a 'trip wire', so causing them to slow down, by which time we would have legged it in all directions!

A friend and I were so keen on playing war as children that we used to regularly crawl through the extremely long grass in his back garden pretending to be Zulu warriors, often with makeshift spears and shields. This play would often last for the entire summer holiday - until one summer when a neighbour opposite complained about the grass being too long and so my friend's parents were forced to cut it down.

As an alternative to my friend's garden we would often walk to a place we called 'Pigs Lane', where we would run through fields with sticks, chopping the heads off tall plants. In reality I think these were actually weeds, but in our imaginations they were man-eating alien triffids, and therefore we were doing the human race a massive favour. An invasion of alien-like plants or not, our heroics were stopped by an irate farmer and his three fierce-looking dogs.

As young teenagers we would regularly hang around our housing estate and sit on some benches, which, during the day, were under the control of the older folk. This became such a routine that on every Friday evening, our stomachs full of chips and curry sauce, and our ghetto blasters in hand, we would camp out for hours until we were either too cold, too tired, or too bored, or until our parents had sent out a search party under the guise of an older sibling. Of course we were often asked to turn our music down, in which case a trip into town would be an alternative adventure - the adventure being to survive without being chased by older teenagers, or to be moved on by the police.

With nowhere else to go, my last remaining images of youth were hanging around a cemetery opposite our housing estate, and while we were rarely asked to leave, there was always a sense that we shouldn't have been there purely out of respect for the deceased.

The issues that emerge from these personal reflections for me now, as an adult working in children's play, are that children will play anywhere and everywhere. Children do not see an environment as having specific pre-requisites for it to be a 'play environment'. In fact, any environment can be suitable for play, as play is not bound to a defined area or space. So even potentially dangerous environments, such as a building site, cattle market or the local cemetery, will be an attractive proposition for children's play.

Children today just don't seem as interested in playing outside as they did when I was a child. This is not because they dislike being outside or dislike playing. No - it is rather that we adults have in some way made it this way.

There is an irony that runs throughout this book, which identifies adults as being largely to blame for impeding children's access to, and interest in, outdoor play. The irony is that change rests largely upon the shoulders of those who caused this difficulty in the first place - us adults. What is perhaps even more ironic is that these adults were once children themselves who probably had greater freedoms to play outside than children have today and therefore should be more in tune with these issues. But no - somehow, somewhere, something has gone terribly wrong.

Today's adults have lost touch with their own personal childhood experiences and have allowed other agendas to supersede them. I do not claim to be an exception to this - I am as much to blame as any other adult. For example, when I see children I know engaging in 'risky' adventures I have, on occasion, allowed my own 'fears' to come into play, or have stopped their playful behaviour because it doesn't suit the 'adult' environment we have been in (think of the supermarket), or have tidied up the rubbish in the back garden because of fears of being reported to the council like my friend's parents were all those years ago. I am guilty as charged!

If we were to be really honest then I think we can all admit that the world we live in is an adult one; a world where children are seen as 'adults in the making' rather than as little people requiring a suitable environment for their 'littleness'. What's more, many of these 'little' people who play outside are increasingly becoming a rarity, a sort of endangered species, with the majority of them being in a state of reliance on adults to provide opportunities for them to play. Moreover, much of this provision will be compensatory - that is, the type of provision we offer compensates for children not being able to access or play in the sorts of environments I have reminisced about above. If this is true, then the very least we can do is provide environments that are more respectful of children's own ideals, and where barriers to accessing certain environments are legitimate, rather than poorly-stated excuses.

Our work with children may often be about creating or designing spaces for children to play in, it may involve managing and resourcing those spaces, and perhaps even staffing them, which is all good stuff if done properly. More than this, however, is how we help children access and engage with **all** spaces that are outside. It is about challenging the attitudes and values of adults towards children playing outside, and finding ways that both adults and children can harmonise with regard to use of external space.

So what 'The Buskers Guide to Playing Out' doesn't do therefore is provide a curriculum or suggest activities for children's outdoor play - the traditional (adult-led) approach. Instead, it addresses two main issues: the first is to explore briefly why 'playing out' is important for children, while the second is how adults can support children's playing outside. Hopefully this will mean that by the end of this book we will all be able to look more creatively at the way we help children to play out.

Philip Waters

The sign on the door reads: "This way for playing out"

Chapter 1
The importance of 'playing out'

Whenever I am teaching a play-based workshop to adult students I often begin with a reflective task that requires them to think back to their own childhoods. This normally includes giving them points of reference - for example, the types of play they may have engaged in, whom they played with, what they played with, but more importantly, where they played. I would say that about 75% of play-memory-recall involves play outside.

What this information tells me is that for many adults 'playing out' offered them some very valuable childhood experiences - so much so, that when you ask these adults to rate the 'importance' of playing outside for themselves as children and for children today it gets quite a massive response, and a positive one at that. Therefore 'playing out' is highly important and that's all we need to know. Hope you've enjoyed this book... Goodbye.

Yeah, right…if only things were that simple!

If 'playing out' is so important, in that we do not believe today's children are getting enough of it, or that what they are getting is of 'poor quality' and as a result we are going to do something about it, then we need to understand what it is that makes it so important. We need to explore playing outside from a number of different viewpoints, which will, I hope, leave you in no doubt about the 'importance' of children playing out.

Inside v outside

We know that children will play anywhere and everywhere, and that many themes played inside can also be played outside. So is there really any difference in children's play based on whether they are indoors or outdoors?

Well, there are some obvious differences, such as the size of the available space for example. Games like football or tag are better suited in large open spaces, so minimising damage to property and players, whereas board games and building with construction toys can be comfortably played in indoor spaces.

Another difference is that large play spaces offer children both a physiological and psychological freedom. They have space to run, climb, roll, jump and move in any and every direction. In addition to movement, they may also have various types of surfaces to physically engage with which would be inaccessible when indoors. For example, sand, water, mud, pebbles, grass, concrete, asphalt and bark chippings all give children variable textures and variable ways of responding to those textures. Or in other words, think of footprints in sand or mud - I guess it would be extremely painful if you attempted stamping a footprint into a wooden floor!

Large spaces outside also leave children being exposed to the elements and anything else that nature may throw their way – including rain drops, snow, hail, leaves, bird droppings, and, during freak weather conditions, frogs!

What is more, some things when presented indoors may be potentially more threatening to children than when outdoors. Take noise, for example. Certain noises inside, such as screaming or shouting, are partially or even fully eradicated when outside, which in itself could be a stress-reducing process.

The outdoors offers children much more scope for altering their play space than do indoor environments - think here about building igloos from snow, or dens from trees and branches, or damming up streams, or making mud hills and sand castles – all can be redesigned and built again.

Indoor and outdoor spaces will bring respective differences to children's overall experiences of play, therefore it is not so much about one being better than the other, but rather, about one being different than the other.

Control of own space

While children can, and do, control indoor spaces, the outdoors tends to favour this control to a much larger degree. Take the school environment, for example. In the classroom children move and operate within the confines of rules and teacher governance. The playground on the other hand should enable children to select where and what they are going to play. It ought to offer children the opportunity to control their own space, but if the space is demarcated for different activities, such as football, hopscotch, skipping, etc, and these areas are excessively controlled by adults, then children will not gain the control they need.

screeech!

Of course we also know that the playground can be difficult sometimes - for example, dominant groups of children who stop others from gaining access to a particular space (older/younger, largest/smallest, boys/girls, juniors/infants). However, the kind of interactions that take place in the playground, particularly where children have a great deal of control, equips many of them with the essential social and mastery skills they will require throughout their lives.

Testing Boundaries

We all know that children will want and need to test boundaries. It's a normal part of development. Playing outdoors enables a child to test certain boundaries in a way that would be unacceptable inside. Outside, children have more chance to use unacceptable language out of adult earshot, or be able to shout as loud as possible, or be able to run without fear of reprimand or of causing damage, whereas most indoor environments tend to magnify these by more readily bringing them to the adult's attention.

Children also create their own boundaries when they play. Some boundaries are physical ones, such as the rectangle shape of a football pitch, with goal posts marked out by jumpers and school bags. Others are imaginary, or in other words, the area that a child may see in their mind's eye - for example, a patch of grass being a rocket launch pad. The outdoors offers children much more scope for creating large and extended boundaries with the greater possibility of negotiating how this bigger space can be demarcated for different types of play, or of how to deal with boundaries that cross over each other.

Different types of resources

It is fairly obvious that some of the resources children play with indoors are going to be different to those they play with outdoors. That is not to say that equipment or toys from inside cannot go outside, or vice versa. Of course they can (and should!). But some resources that are outdoors are always going to remain there and therefore are always going to offer something different to children as far as playing is concerned. Take tree climbing, for example. No manufactured climbing frame - either indoors or outdoors - is going to be as exciting, variable and challenging as a real tree, just as the sand and water tray is never going to replace the explorations to be had if playing at the seaside. Besides, you cannot comfortably keep seaweed, limpets and crabs in the kitchen sink!

Novelty

Do you ever find that gruesome or bizarre news stories on the television attract your attention, or that a new craze or fad grabs your curiosity? Perhaps you are a devil for buying the latest gadget for the kitchen, or a tool for the shed? Anyway, if you do then the chances are that you are in tune with your neophilic drive.

Neo...what!

Neophilia is about children's curiosity for the novel and the strange. The neophilic effect on one child may therefore be very different from that on another. For example, one child may find every new pebble or shell they find on a beach very exciting - particularly if they rarely frequent such an environment, whereas the child who perhaps lives near the coast may have exhausted that particular interest.

Outdoor play environments are particularly nourishing for neophilia, especially for those who have an interest

in historical or archaeological facts, or treasure hunts, as the neophilic drive kicks in even before the 'treasure' is found. Neophilia is like a drug that induces anticipation of finding something, where the outcome of a treasure found is less important than the anticipation itself. My dad knew this all too well, as he used to hide coins in a garden allotment so we would dig it over for him before planting. Of course, we were looking for treasure while all he wanted was the allotment dug. I now wonder if it wouldn't have been much quicker for him to turn the soil himself considering the time he must have spent hiding the coins!

Playscapes

When children play, especially types of fantasy or imaginative play, they will project their internal thoughts into the play space, into the real physical environment. For example, think of children playing 'dragon-slayers' - the grassy bank may represent a volcanic mountain, and the tree a dragon, so the environment and props within that space become symbolic of what is in the child's imagination.

The imagery that is representative of an environment is what could be called an inscape - a landscape that is inside your head. It could be a memory of a landscape you know well, or have visited, or could equally be a hotchpotch of many landscapes or environments. The great thing about children holding these sorts of backdrops for their play is that they do not necessarily have to be playing near an actual volcano or an actual dragon. The whole purpose of using the inscape is to account for the fact that the actual environment they are playing in bears no resemblance to the one they need. It is a way for the child to be someplace 'in essence', without actually being there physically.

Thinking about spaces as being within the child's mind helps us to appreciate that it is not simply a case of a child and an environment, but a very deep and subtle interaction between the two, with external 'landscapes' offering the child a platform for some rather elaborate and imagined environments.

You can get an impression of an inscape by finding a quiet space to sit and attempt to visualise an environment you often frequent. What sorts of images come to mind? Can you make mental changes to that environment? Can you move objects about? Can you add new parts, so creating a very new and different environment?

Developing an identity

It is probably not that easy to make a tangible connection between children's play outside and that of a child developing an identity - after all, surely children gain information about their self in relation to others in whatever context they find themselves, indoors or outdoors? This is certainly true. However, the outdoor environment does lend itself rather well to some types of self-development which are different to those available from playing indoors.

For example, think of gangs. It seems to me that at the point children become young people a most remarkable and sometimes alarming change takes place. The sweet, angelic nature of the child dramatically fades and a ruthless, ear-pierced, smoking, swearing, alco-pop-drinking creature emerges from within. Okay, you spotted the slight exaggeration, but I think you'll agree that they certainly do change!

Young people get to a stage in their development where they want to be independent from their primary carer, whilst at the same time begin to seek a dependency within a peer group of similar status. It is a very natural process and one that cannot be avoided by enlisting children into academies, clubs or organised groups. It

just doesn't work like that. Yes, young people have an urge to be part of a social group, but the group is normally one of their own choosing. And hanging about on the street, at the beach, or in the local telephone box are the sorts of places that enable their autonomy.

Housing estates, and the outdoor space provided by the arrangement of houses and land, are beneficial to children learning social rules and cultural values. For example, many children growing up on housing estates tend to stick together with their own 'housing estate group'. So, should a child from another housing estate wander into their 'territory' they would rarely be made welcome. Or, worse than that, would be to make friends with one of the 'enemy', which is often seen as a treacherous act and can leave the 'traitor' to be completely alienated from their own housing-estate 'tribe'.

Likewise, when children are left to their own devices, for example, in the school playground, they can learn a lot about themselves and those around them. Playground culture acts like a miniature version of the wider society to which they belong, with play operating as the conduit through which they communicate. Any outside play space is therefore a laboratory for learning and practising social skills.

Natural urges?

Do you ever feel the urge to get out of the house or workplace and enjoy the fresh air? If so, would you rather it was in a natural, unspoiled environment? If you answered yes to these questions, then you are partly biophilic.

Bio…who?

Biophilia simply means that we have a love or passion for the natural world, and yes, biophobia means completely the opposite, that we have a hate or disinterest for the natural world.

All of the natural world is outdoors, so when children play in the woods, near a river, in a field, at the beach, in the mud, go looking for animals or insects, climb trees or dam up streams, they are displaying a biophilic tendency. Moreover, this relationship with the natural world is a very important one, in that by maintaining links with it we are more likely to look after it and so aid our own continued survival. After all, if we chop down all the trees and pollute the entire atmosphere then eventually we are all going to become extinct!

Within play this process serves a very important function as it encourages children to access natural environments and so experience and learn more about the world than they would find from a textbook or in a classroom.

Biophobia, on the other hand, could mean that we do not take care of the environment and so let it go to ruin - but no, it is actually nature's way of maintaining itself. If we have a fear of creepy jungles, for example, or of the creatures that roam within them, such as spiders and crocodiles, then we are less likely to want to adventure into them and so they can remain undisturbed and perhaps preserved.

Ranging

Some species, like large predatory cats for example, have what is called a 'home range' - that is, a defined space or territory that they use for hunting. They tend to mark their territory with scent so that other cats do not invade their space. Us humans are really not that much different when it comes to demarcating territory or operating within a range (think about the garden fence which separates you from the rest of the world).

When they are born children have a very limited range. They are first connected to their primary carer and their range very slowly increases as they become more independent. So by the time the child becomes a young person, their range can be most of their local neighbourhood and even beyond. Playing out helps a child to increase his or her range and also increase the experiences gained from ranging. For example, children playing tag games on the street may gain confidence in stretching the game into new streets each time they play the game, and therefore the thrill and excitement of playing in 'new territories' add to the gradual extending of the child's range.

Ranging allows the child to extend both physical and psychological boundaries - that is, by exploring further away from the base environment the child grows more confident as an individual. So as a child's range increases, so does their confidence and independence.

Physical Health

In recent years there has been a tremendous surge in public interest in the health of children. We are constantly being bombarded with research and medical reports that suggest today's children are increasingly becoming unhealthy and unfit, with obesity and related illnesses reaching huge proportions. Some of the suggested remedies for this have been to add nutritional value to children's diets, especially in schools, and to encourage children to adopt a more physical and healthy lifestyle.

Play outside naturally lends itself to children's capacity to engage in physical exertion, as the outdoors is a haven for resources and spaces that lend themselves to children engaging in physical forms of play that will naturally keep them fit. In fact play in its own right can maintain the physical health of children - could children therefore regulate their own fitness levels more effectively if they are able to play outside more?

Psychological health

Perhaps what is less explored is the impact that outdoor play has on children's psychological well-being. For example, we know that certain weather climates have a deep and far-reaching affect on us - just consider Seasonal Affective Disorder (SAD). What's more, it is not only the sun that makes us feel good, but also being in an environment during a thunderstorm, or where there is a heavy downpour of rain, or where there is snow - all have the potential to exhilarate us, to stimulate our senses. All these things tap into a hidden part of our consciousness and promote therapeutic qualities – a sort of healing from within. Play is a vehicle through which a form of healing can take place and the outdoors is the therapeutic space.

Playing in a natural environment has the added benefit of utilising nature's backdrop as a therapeutic setting, as the outdoors has much more of a 'symphony' to offer the child's ears than does the indoor world - think of wildlife, trickling streams and swaying trees. What's more, think of all the sound recordings used for meditation and you realise that they are all taken from outdoor environments.

Playing Out

It seems to me that there is a wealth of reasons why children and young people ought to be playing out. Now at this stage I could suggest that you leave a few doors open and see what happens! But you probably know as well as I do that it requires just a little more creativity, especially when working in supervised play settings. The next three chapters are therefore about exploring what it is that you and I can do to support and actively encourage children's playing out.

Chapter 2
Play Spaces

Look out of your window.

Go on, take a peek; you know you want to.

What do you see? What do you see out there that could be defined as adult space? In other words, what do you see through your adult eyes?

Okay, let's try this a different way. If I asked you to take a walk down a street, any street, then no doubt most of what you see will primarily be for us grown-ups - for example, roads, cars, shops, restaurants, golf courses, bowling greens, houses, etc. We really do live in an adult world.

Take another peek - but this time I want you to consider what is out there for children. What would you see if you were to look through the eyes of a child? See anything different? I am guessing there's not a lot. We adults are very quick to define our own spaces, but even quicker to define what is not for children - and even those areas we do define as being 'for children' are still really ours. Shops have signs that say 'children to be accompanied by an adult', grass areas on housing estates say 'no ball games' and side streets say 'this is not a children's play area'.

Let's be honest, there really are no spaces out there that are truly for children. Or are there?

Play Environment

What exactly is a play environment?
If you were to imagine that the blank page opposite had a picture of a 'play environment', what would your play environment look like? What sorts of things would you see in your play environment? Perhaps you'd like to sketch one?

Ok, so what sorts of things popped into your head? I suspect that you were thinking about parks, adventure playgrounds or school playgrounds? Perhaps they had areas of tarmac or grass, or with some fixed equipment like slides, climbing frames, swings, etc. Am I right? No worries if I'm not, sometimes I get these things wrong...

Play Space

So what if this time I asked you not to think of a 'play environment', but rather, a 'play space'? What would your play space look like? What sorts of things would you see in your play space?

Any new ideas emerge? Or did you find it more difficult to visualise a play space than a play environment? As I said, no worries if you did, it's not a test.

It seems to me that there is quite a difference between a 'play environment' and a 'play space'. A play environment suggests an area that has been 'designated' for children's play. In many ways this suggests that someone, somewhere, is saying 'this space is for children and children only'. We know all too well, however, that rarely is a place, designated or not, just for children. But the idea is a nice one nevertheless. And perhaps even a step in the right direction.

However, if we think of the term 'space' - and no, I don't envisage sending all children to the moon, although now you come to think of it… sorry, my children were playing up (rather than out) this morning - where was I? Ah, yes, if we were to think of a 'play space', then we are actually not designating any specific area as being for children's play, we are actually saying that any space (and yes, perhaps even on the moon) is potentially a space where children can play. What's more, by simply reframing how we think about the spaces that children can use for play, we are actually moving away from seeing the world as purely an adult one.

So what does this have to do with the children you work with?

Good question. Well, I suspect that many of you are working with children so that their play is 'supervised'. Therefore my guess is that you will also be enabling children to access some form of outdoor space.

Now some of you may be fortunate in that you have lots of outdoor space of various shapes, sizes, styles and textures all provided free and gratis by Mother Nature. You may also have the added luxury of hard areas, soft areas, movable areas, quiet areas, hiding areas, climbing areas, wet areas, dry areas, grass areas, tarmac areas, muddy areas, sandy areas, ball areas, rope areas, game areas, and crater areas... sorry, still on the moon! In reality, however, I am predicting that many of you have limited access to an outdoor play area, or a 'perceived' outdoor play area.

However, I am going to challenge you on this thinking because I think you do have access to outdoor play areas - and quite a variety of them too. It's just I think that we don't see them as outdoor play areas. I say this because a 'play space' can be any space outdoors, and not necessarily a space designated for children's use.

A play space can be the pavement outside your home, it can be the teachers' car park at the school, it can be the path that separates your school playground from the housing estate next door, or the muddy track that acts as a boundary between your setting and the farmer's field - it may even be the farmer's field if you ask him kindly for access. Of course you need to get the right permissions/do the risk assessments/get the space registered (please delete as applicable!). But we also need to take a creative approach and remember that children can, and do, when left to their own devices, play anywhere and everywhere. Therefore any outdoor space is a potential play space to a child.

Built Spaces

As much as we like to see children access natural environments, which we'll explore in just a moment, it is also important for us to enable children to access and play in and around the built environment - that is, man-made structures.

The most obvious built structures regarding children's play are typically found on playgrounds, for example, swings, slides, round-a-bouts, etc. However, not everyone has immediate access to a purpose-built playground, with those who do often finding them in a state of disrepair. In addition we have to question what

sort of play value these built play spaces have for children's play, particularly if children have had no say in their design, or they are placed too far from a child's home range.

Informal play spaces within a built environment can be varied and challenging. For example, in recent years a craze has swept both the USA and Europe whereby young people climb on and leap off different parts of buildings. I am not suggesting that you send children to the top of ten-storey buildings and encourage them to take a leap of faith! Instead, let's think about whether we actually need to discourage children when they engage with structures in a way that was not originally intended - for example, children climbing walls in your setting, or spinning around handrails, or bumping down steps on a skateboard, or chalking pictures and symbols on a pavement, or building their own structures from bricks and mortar.

Sure, we need to make certain that we have risk-assessed these playful uses of the built environment, just as we need to put in appropriate safety measures. But we also need to think creatively about how children can access and engage with a built space, rather than how they cannot – just because something was not designed for children to play with, doesn't mean that it is automatically dangerous and should therefore be 'banned'.

Natural spaces

The natural environment, whilst it does have certain access issues similar to the built environment, has a wider variety of resources and spaces to explore, including the capacity to change and adapt with climate and seasonal cycles. For example, rivers and streams continuously flow, trees and shrubs never stop growing, and animals and insects roam and settle wherever they feel like it. What's more, we are really not alone as a species when we are playing in the natural world, so it is important for adults and children alike to consider sharing spaces with other creatures and having some consideration for their habitats.

Landscapes offered within natural spaces tend to be far more inspiring than those offered within built spaces, and I think you'll agree that 'nature' is by far a better architect than most humans. However, access to these spaces is just as challenging as children playing in built spaces. For example, transportation to and from the beach, or moor, or woodland, and the capacity to engage with props within these natural spaces, such as trees, rivers, and large rocks, are of course usually governed by the adult world.

For some settings, access to large and open natural spaces may be a real barrier. However, smaller natural spaces may just as well do the trick. You could find children a small patch of ground to dig in, bury in, plant flowers and vegetables, or of course make mud pies! You could also let children clamber in the bushes and make dens, or climb a nearby tree, or even make a rockery. How about even getting some pebbles, shells and a few bags of sand to make an artificial beach, or some earth, stones and plant-life to make a miniature garden if something on a grander scale cannot be accessed?

Indigenous Play Spaces

Close your eyes.

I know, I am always asking you to do something, but this is a good exercise, so close your eyes.
Ok, perhaps you ought to read the rest of this paragraph first and then close your eyes!

At the beginning of this chapter I asked you to look at the difference between a play environment and a play space - a play space being 'any space' children may want to use for their play. This time see if you can imagine an 'ideal' play space.

❖ What would it look like?
❖ Where is it?
❖ How do children engage with this space?

I wonder if your imagined 'ideal' play space looks like something dreamed up by adults or something dreamed up by children?

An ideal play space - inside or outside, built or natural - would be one that is indigenous to children – or in other words, for and by children. In this space children's play is highly valued and respected. It would not be defined by those in power, or those who could afford to pay for it, or those who managed it, or those who designed it, or even those who built it. Instead, it would belong to children.

So how can you get yourself one of these spaces then?

Well, you could try buying one, but they tend to come 'ready made', which kind of defeats the purpose really. The only way to get an indigenous play space is by involving the children in its design, construction, management and use.

So you could ask children in your setting what their ideal outdoor play space would look like. For example, could they design this space? Could you support them in creating it? If you have a limited budget can you get sponsorship to create this space? Can you get specialised help from parents to create this space? Can you get resources cheap or perhaps even free by contacting local businesses and offering publicity? If sharing or renting premises with other users, can you get support from them? More importantly, does this space have the capacity to be continually changed or adapted by the children themselves so they maintain ownership over it? Whatever you do, it must include the children.

Trips and outings

If creating outdoor play spaces is a real difficulty, then you can still help children to 'play out' by providing trips and outings.

It is often assumed that a trip is going to be a costly ordeal, and therefore many settings avoid them. Well, some trips may very well be expensive, particularly those to theme parks and the like, but there are many other alternative environments worth considering, including the beach, the moor, the woods, a forest, a field, a lake, the local park, a local grassy area, the town centre, a garden (public or private), a skateboard park, a

river, a stream, a rocky area, a country lane, a disused quarry, a disused warehouse or building, a disused railway track, an adventure playground, a pedestrian-only street, a barn, a mobile play unit, the drain covers in a playground, or the cracks in a pavement somewhere etc, etc, etc…

The choices are endless and it's probably the case sometimes that adults are only restricted by their own imaginations and ingenuity. For example, one playscheme I know of used to get permission from a local farmer to access a field that was on a steep hill. If not swinging from a rope attached to a tree, children would roly-poly through the long grass. I also know of a school that gave up a patch of grass to a number of local playschemes so that the children could play there.

Playing Out in a Play Space

Okay, on looking out of the window we see that children will play just about anywhere and everywhere and that any space can be a play space. We also know that children need to access both built and natural spaces, and that a 'good' play space is one that is indigenous to children. Oh, and trips are another way of helping children to play outside. Right, now that's all sorted perhaps you'd like to open the door instead?

Yes? Well, before we get too excited perhaps we could think about putting some objects out there for children to play with. So come with me, we're going to chapter three!

Chapter 3
Play Stuff

How many uses can you think of for a brick?

Just as children will play anywhere and everywhere, they will also play with anything and everything - including manufactured toys, natural materials, junk, the neighbour's dog, and even (unfortunately!) the mess that the neighbour's dog leaves behind on the roadside! Whatever the artefact, large or small, hard or soft, clean or smelly, children will find some use for it within their play. So, this chapter is about children's use of objects whilst playing out and the sorts of things that adults can do to support this.

So how many uses do you have for a brick? I have 28!

Lots of 'stuff'

When thinking about providing resources for children playing out, have a go at thinking about 'stuff' instead. Thinking about 'stuff', rather than resources, means that you consider just about any object or artefact as being usable in children's play; bricks, stones, leaves, wood, pipes, cushions, cardboard tubes, pebbles, sand, chairs, water, earth, food and - well just about anything really - except the mess from the neighbour's dog!

Children will of course use whatever 'stuff' they find in their play space and therefore we can see how the environment defines what they play with. However, adults working with children should ensure that the 'stuff' does not only come from one type of environment – or in other words, we need to provide stuff in our settings that belong to both the indoor and the outdoor world.

Manufactured Stuff

Lots of settings will have easy access to man-made 'stuff'. Of course, not all the stuff that the children play with will be toys (after all, manufactured objects can include egg cartons, settee cushions, plastic cups, concrete blocks etc).

Adults who work with children need to carefully consider what types of stuff are available to children in their outdoor environments - and more importantly, what is not. For example, are children able to take manufactured stuff, perhaps usually kept indoors, outside? If not, why not? Ok, the settee may not comfortably fit through the door, but most other things will.

If given half the chance children will introduce all sorts of objects into their outdoor play. It is worth remembering therefore that some objects can represent something the child cannot have or access in reality - for example, a broom could be a horse, or a cardboard box a car, or a brick a walkie-talkie (that's 29 uses I have now!). Therefore access to all sorts of manufactured stuff is important, so that children get as much out of their outdoor play space as possible.

Can you list a range of manufactured stuff in your setting that children can use in their play outside? And (sorry to repeat myself) if not, why not?

Natural Stuff

As with manufactured stuff, some
environments offer certain natural
resources that support particular
play themes or particular ways of
playing. Consider the beach, for
example. Natural resources found
here, like the sea, sand, shells,
pebbles, and aquatic life forms etc,
could predict that a child's play will
involve digging and burying themes,
collecting themes, construction and
destruction themes (sand castles), and other forms of
exploratory play. Therefore the space and resources
when combined together can give children an idea
about how to play.

There are of course four natural resources that are
readily available in most outdoor spaces and yet are
rarely considered as something for children to play with
- the four elements.

For the most part each of the four elements provide
opportunities for lots of different ways of playing. I
know, you are probably already squirming in your seats
at the thought of children engaging with fire, but I am
not asking you to give a four-year-old a flame-thrower,
just as I am not asking you to throw a seven-year-old

into the river! Of course adults need to risk assess all types of play for the children that they are working with – whilst also remembering that children have a remarkable talent at recognising their own limitations and capabilities.

Playing with the elements ranges from flying kites to windsurfing; building igloos to dancing in the rain; making mud pies to lounging in a mud hole; cooking food over a campfire to burning objects with a magnifying glass. Children are easily drawn to the four elements – it seems crazy therefore to think that children would not want to engage with them, or that some adults would not allow it!

Consumable Stuff

Playing out, just like playing inside, relies on those resources that can be used only once, or in other words, 'consumable' stuff.

There's no need to explore this deeply as I am sure you can list many resources that are consumable, such as paper, paint, cardboard boxes, most art and craft materials, foods, etc, etc. While these resources can and are used outdoors, there are also some resources particular to outdoor environments that can also be considered consumable, for example, earth, water, twigs, leaves, plants, flowers, and weeds, etc. The biggest consideration for children and adults when selecting consumable resources outdoors is using those that are safe for children to play with (non-poisonous plants, for example) and those that are already perishing (leavesand branches that have already fallen from trees) and of course, avoiding rare flowers!

Flexible Stuff

We all know that children will sometimes play with objects that typically go together - for example, play-dough modelling requires shape cutters, a rolling pin and a table-top. We also know that children will play with objects that appear to be unrelated. Thus, allow children to use a telephone, a tree and a cardboard box all together and hey presto! - an intergalactic teleportation device!

Surprising though these combinations of objects can seem, children's development often relies on such experimentation.

Therefore adults always need to be careful that they do not limit children's creativity. In fact, adults ought to be encouraging children's play with objects wherever possible, perhaps by supplying 'unrelated' objects in storage containers together so that children can feel at ease in playing with them – for example, bits of fabric with cricket bats, hoses from vacuum cleaners with ping-pong balls, and string with sand.

It can be interesting to see how children combine different objects in their outdoor play. For example, at one playscheme children lined a hole with some bin-liners, filled it with water, sat in it, removed the bags, made some mud, sat in it again, put a plank of wood over it, jumped off the plank into the mud, got all their friends to stand in the mud, etc, etc. Whilst this may challenge our adult fears about cleanliness, behaviour and safety, it only goes to show that when children are left to their own devices in combining objects they can come to no harm and have a great time!

Novel stuff

As we saw in Chapter 1, children are inspired and intrigued by things that are odd. This is especially true of objects they have never seen before, or even where they have, they have not been able or allowed to engage with.

Most settings need to keep this in mind when stocking up on resources. So rather than getting stuff you have available all the time, perhaps try something different each time you make an order or request for stock. For example, I know of a setting that keeps a trunk full of broken video recorders, radios, watches, clocks, telephones and the like so that children can engage with items they do not typically have the opportunity to do so elsewhere.

Another setting used to stock water woggles and pipe insulation tubes; not because they were keen swimmers or needed to insulate their heating pipes, but because the children would either use them as padded swords in rough and tumble play or as cushioned support poles for fabric-based dens built outside, so when the den collapsed the whole experience would be a gentle one.

Now I'd build my den with bricks, at least one hundred of them…

…In which case that's 129 uses I have for a brick!

Playing Out with Play Stuff

Ok, we could just say here 'get lots of stuff for your setting'. And it's true that children do need lots of stuff to play with when they are outside. But we now know that it's not quite as simple as that, because we need to think about getting different types of stuff –

manufactured stuff, natural stuff, consumable stuff and unusual stuff. And when we've done that, we also need to think about how we can encourage children to combine this stuff in different ways and how we can support children in doing this. And that's in chapter four…

Chapter 4
Come out and play!

So far then, we've looked at why it's important for children to play outside, and how in enabling this to happen we have to think about where children play and what they play with. I really would like you to come out and play now, but just before we do, we need to look at the importance of risk and risk-assessment in children's play outside. Finally, we need to prepare the space and stuff so that children can get on with playing – and *then* we can join them!

Riskogenics

I hope you don't mind but now would be a good time for me to plug a new business venture I am starting called ALPC- Anti-Ludic Protective Clothing for children; a franchise of Child Protective Systems™.

Yes, our latest range of technical clothing includes Treeclimber™ basic, a fully padded jumpsuit which comes with an integral safety net and telescopic ladder, so no more worries about a child's first tentative reach for that branch. Of course the deluxe Treeclimber comes with padded rear end to make children's branch sitting as comfortable as possible.

For adults concerned about children getting lost then we of course have the Rangefinder™ uniforms. Rangefinder 1 comes complete with integral homing beacon so should a child's ranging go beyond a set boundary then our patented radar tracking system will automatically detect and deploy a Rangefinder officer. Rangefinder 2 has the added luxury of an electric fence for your property that comes in all sizes, but for the truly conscientious adult, Rangefinder 2 comes with ten pairs of deadweight magnetised boots which will pin your child to the spot when the alarm is triggered.

Clothing comes with the anti-ludic technology as standard and a full-money back guarantee.

It may seem ludicrous, but how far are we away from companies like ALPC actually existing? And how far are we prepared to go before we say enough is enough?

Let's be honest, some of us adults go out of our way to ensure that there are certain experiences children do not have. A few of these are necessary, like protecting children from abuse or from exposure to drugs. But let's have a look at some of the other – perhaps more questionable – areas where adults get involved. Take tree climbing, for example. In all honesty, how often do you hear about a child becoming seriously injured or even die as a result of falling out of a tree? It is extremely rare.

Trees, like embankments, rocks, rivers, ropes over rivers, rafts on rivers, or even homemade submarines under rivers, are the sorts of things that children do and want to engage in when they are outside playing. We need to make sure that we are supporting children's play outside rather than impeding it.

Children do need to take risks when they play. That's not to say you give a five-year-old a sharp knife and leave them unsupervised while cutting through a branch - that would be daft! Instead, we should be looking at ways that children can access potentially risky outdoor play experiences. If we are carrying out risk assessments on the space, resources and the way that children play, then we can enable, rather than disable, children's risk-taking opportunities.

Comfort zones

So having just said, 'go on, help children take some risks', my guess is that some of you are now squirming in your chair again while thinking about the wrath of a parent being brought down upon you from some great height! Play is, it's true, both a risky business and a scary business, and sometimes this means that we have to be prepared to move out of our own comfort zones to enable children to play.

So what exactly is so scary about children taking risks or indeed, about us helping them to experience risks?

❖ Is it that we are certain that the children are going to come to some physical harm? If that were a certainty then we would have to have a remarkable talent for foreseeing the future!

❖ Or is it that we are certain that they are going to come to some psychological harm? If so, perhaps we are more easily spooked than the children, just because of our own fears. For example, how many people who don't like heights display this fear to children, even sub-consciously?

When working with children we all need to work 'consciously'. That is, we need to be constantly listening to ourselves, constantly questioning every thought and idea that goes on inside our heads. In doing this we are checking that we don't unintentionally pass our own fears onto children, or stop them from taking risks that *we* see as 'too risky' but could well be, in fact, appropriate for that particular child. We should, in short, carry out a risk assessment of our own thoughts as much as we do of a play space, or play stuff, or the way that children play. And when we do our risk assessments, sometimes we find ourselves left with different comfort zones!

'Can Do'

Another part of risk assessing children's outdoor play is to try wherever possible to convert a 'can't do' attitude to a 'can do' one - which, as some wise old person once told me, simply involved removing the letter 't'!

Can you remove the 't' from the following examples?
❖ Can't play in the rain because you'll get wet
❖ Can't play on the concrete steps in case you hurt yourself

A 'can do' approach to the above situations may offer solutions such as; giving children waterproof clothing and shoes, providing towels, or additional clothing while playing in the rain. It could also involve talking with children beforehand to see if they are aware of the hazards involved in playing on steps, and what they can do to reduce the risks of hurting themselves. A 'can do' approach helps us to assess whether it is simply our comfort zones which are being challenged or whether indeed the risks are actually too great for the children we are working with. Besides, it's easy to say 'no', but far more challenging and interesting to find solutions that allow you to say 'yes'.

Preparation of space

So how else can you support children playing out? Well, one way is to prepare the space they are going to play in.

At its simplest level preparation of the play space is about carrying out health and safety checks – you know, checking grass areas for needles, broken glass, and animal excrement. It is also about checking equipment for damages.

Preparation of the play space may also involve the setting up of fixed or mobile equipment. Whilst this seems fairly simple, sometimes it may actually require a lot of thinking about. For example, you may be preparing the play space to accentuate a theme at a child's request - like a 'dragon's lair'. Or, instead of responding to direct requests, you might have observed children having to leave the setting just as they were about to 'slay the dragon'. In which case you are setting up the 'dragon's lair' just as it was when they left, so that they can return to their adventure if they choose.

Setting up the space may also involve preparing it in a way the children may never have experienced before so that they can experience new ways of engaging with the environment - for example, pouring water into a ditch so as to make a mud pit which children could get in and get dirty! Or how about putting some dressing-up

WHIRRR

CAUTION
GRASS
HOOVERING
IN
PROGRESS

clothes underneath the climbing frame and seeing what happens?

Some preparations of the play space may involve transformations on a much bigger scale, such as landscaping the space in new and exciting ways. To do this we need to adopt the playful perspective of a child and that involves knowing how children play in different types of outdoor spaces. This may involve moving away from the 'traditional' demarcated playground with its ball areas, skipping areas, and hopscotch areas, and creating a space that better represents what children want and need when they play. One school did this by introducing small tarmac hillocks into the playground - the children enjoyed playing in new ways on this very uneven play space.

Preparation of outdoor play spaces generally happens, of course, before children enter them.

Sometimes however we will be helping children to make changes to the space while they are in it, perhaps shifting large objects, or trimming bushes, or tying ropes to branches of trees. If we are to do this effectively we have to be mindful that we are actually doing what children want, and not what we think they want – which, as I said earlier, means being conscious of what is going on in our heads as well as what is going on in the space.

Preparation of stuff

Another way that adults can support children's outdoor play is to consider what stuff children may want or need in their outdoor play spaces, what stuff they may never have played with before, and how you can support them in the use of these objects.

For example, if adults were to continually define the uses of certain objects, like instructing children to use objects in a specific way, then children's natural curiosity to explore through their play with objects will become stifled. Adults therefore need to be very attentive to observing how children use objects during play so as not to criticise or make fun of them. The adult saying to a child, who is riding around the grass area on their horse, 'you can't use a broom for that, it's silly', could potentially stop that child from ever engaging with a broom in that way again.

Sometimes it is worth experimenting when preparing stuff for outdoor play, for example;

❖ Putting objects together because they form a natural partnership

❖ Putting random objects together to see if children will invent new uses for them

❖ Putting unusual or novel objects out which children may have never seen, or had access to before

❖ Allowing children to use some objects in ways they were not intended for

❖ Allowing and helping children to take stuff typically for inside, outside, and vice versa.

Who's directing?

Do you know that you are a pretty good resource for children's play?

No, I don't mean children wheeling you out of a cupboard and switching you on when they want to play with you! But if we know our stuff with regard to children's play, and act sensitively and responsively to children's requests to play with them, then the adult can be a very useful play resource indeed.

Being a resource in children's play may involve you acting in a number of different ways - for example, being a 'horse' by pulling children along on a go-kart, or refereeing a game of football, or being a character in a child's fantasy play like the blue-spotted, green-haired, one-eyed gurgle-bug!

Generally, however, the principles of being a resource for children's play are one and the same: let children direct you, rather than you direct them. This doesn't mean of course that children won't welcome suggestions from adults about ideas or even want us to organise games and activities – it just means that we have to make sure that the direction of the play is always under the control of the child.

Reflective practice

Another way of checking that we are acting sensitively and responsively is to use reflective practice – or in other words, to stop for a moment and ask ourselves some basic questions to ensure that children's play outside belongs to them, rather than to us. These questions are;

1. **Where** do children want to play outside today?
2. **What** do children want to play with outside today?
3. **Who** do children want to play with outside today?
4. **How** do children want to play outside today?

These questions help us to check our assumptions about children playing out. Of course, the very fact that you are influencing the where, the what and the who already means that you will have an impact on the how. However, it is important to make sure that this is as far as we go when it comes to influencing the nature of playing out, unless of course there are crucial health and safety issues involved. In other words, we can think about how children will want to play in the space that we have provided for them, but it is children who ultimately need to provide the answer to question four.

Adopting a playful disposition

Did you know that adults were once children? Shocking isn't it?! But when helping children to play outside, it is important to remember that adults generally were once a lot smaller, younger, and more importantly, playful.

An example of a playful approach could be the way you respond to children at play. For example, if a child playing in a sandpit turned to you and said, "There's a giant lobster hiding in here!" and you responded, "That's nice dear, but don't get dirty", then you are not really responding very playfully. If instead you said, "Oh my goodness, will it get out and nip my toes?" Then chances are the child will take up your response and continue to play with you.

Likewise, if a child suggests to you that a rope hanging from a tree is a dangerous alien species and that when they come back to your setting tomorrow they are going to save the world by capturing it, but the following day you haven't arranged to hang the rope back up, then you've potentially killed the 'alien species' on their behalf!

Adopting a playful approach will help you to view the world through children's eyes. So go on, take a look out of the window for one last time. Wouldn't you rather be playing out?!

Bibliography/Further Reading

Bilton, H. (2004) *Playing Outside*. London: David Fulton Publishers.

Bishop, C. and Curtis, M. (ed.) (2001) *Play today in the primary school playground*. Buckingham: Open University Press.

Children's Play Council (2002) *More than swings and roundabouts - planning for outdoor play*. London: National Children's Bureau.

Else, P. and Sturrock, G. (2003) *The Play Cycle - An introduction to Psycholudics*. Eastleigh: Common Threads Publications.

Newstead, S. (2004) *The Buskers Guide to Playwork*. Eastleigh: Common Threads Publications Ltd.

Greenman, J. (1988) *Caring spaces, Learning Places - Children's Environments That Work*. Redmond, WA: Exchange Press Inc.

Hodgson, J. and Dyer, A. (2003) *Let your children go back to nature*. Somerset: Capall Bann Publishing.

Hughes, B. (1996) *Play Environments - A question of quality*. London: PLAYLINK.

Kahn, P.H. and Kellert, S.R. (ed.) (2002) *Children and Nature*. London: MIT Press.

Kaplan, R. and Kaplan, S. (1989) *The experience of nature*. Cambridge: Cambridge University Press.

Krause, B. (2002) *Wild Soundscapes - Discovering the voice of the natural world.* Berkeley: Wilderness Press.

Maudsley, M. (ed.) (2005) *Playing on the wild side*. Gloucestershire: Playwork Partnerships.

Melville, S. (2004) *Places for Play*. London: PLAYLINK.

Nicholson, S. (1971) How not to cheat children: the theory of Loose Parts. *Landscape Architecture, (pp.30-34).*

PLAYLINK (1999) *Reared in Captivity – restoring the freedom to play*. London: PLAYLINK/Portsmouth City Council.

Smith, A. (1994) *Creative outdoor work with young people*. Dorset: Russell House Publishing.

Waters, P. (2005) Free Range - Compound Flexibility. *Out of School*: Nursery World (pp.8-9).

Waters, P. (2005) Back to Nature - Environmental Play. *Out of School*: Nursery World (pp.8-9).